Did You Catch It?

Developing Skills in Listening

Mitaka Yoneda
Chris Valvona

JN116651

CENGAGE
Learning™

Did You Catch It?—Developing Skills in Listening

Mitaka Yoneda and Chris Valvona

© 2012 Cengage Learning K.K.

Photo Credits:
p.15: (left) © Bob Thomas/Getty Images, (right) © Bongarts/Getty Images;
p.17: © Jupiterimages/Thinkstock;
p.29: © iStockphoto/Thinkstock;
p.41: © iStockphoto/Thinkstock;
p.53: © Hemera/Thinkstock;
p.57: © WireImage;
p.63: © Digital Vision/Thinkstock;
p.65: © Hemera/Thinkstock;
p.77: © Ablestock.com/Thinkstock;
p.89: © Jupiterimages/Thinkstock

For permission to use material from this textbook or product, e-mail to **eltjapan@cengage.com**

ISBN: 978-4-86312-214-7

Cengage Learning K.K.
No 2 Funato Building 5th Floor
1-11-11 Kudankita, Chiyoda-ku
Tokyo 102-0073
Japan

Tel: 03-3511-4392
Fax: 03-3511-4391

Preface

As you will see when you reach Unit 13 (The Purpose of Language), we have strong feelings about what it means to learn a language. Of course, it is important to study hard, learning grammar, structure, and vocabulary.

However, it is also very important to actually find ways of putting the language you learn to use. In each unit of this textbook, we hope you will find texts that are interesting, relevant, and stimulating, and that you will be able to use these as a springboard to lively discussion with your classmates.

Furthermore, we hope the activities within each unit that ask you to listen to texts, reproduce what you hear, summarize the information, as well as many other tasks, will provide you with opportunities to put your language abilities to use, as well as hone skills that will likely be very valuable in your future careers.

Most of all, we hope you will enjoy using the book as much as we enjoyed writing it.

本書は、大学生の皆さんに興味を持っていただけるよう、各ユニットで国内外の文化、スポーツ、社会、教育、環境に関する内容を取り上げています。リスニング力の向上に加え、海外での出来事に対する皆さんの関心が深まり、英語の学習意欲がさらに高まることを願っています。

Acknowledgements:

This textbook is for Ayano—your unending support and eagle eye for detail make everything easy. Thank you.

本書を作成するにあたり多くの先生方から貴重なアドバイスを頂戴しました。会議通訳者の砂場裕理氏には通訳訓練法についてご助言をいただきました。この場をお借りして御礼申し上げます。また、本書出版に際し、企画の段階からご尽力くださいましたセンゲージ ラーニングの吉田剛氏に感謝の意を表します。

Mitaka Yoneda and Chris Valvona

Table of Contents

本書の構成と効果的な使い方

●ユニットの基本的な学習の流れ

各ユニットの学習は、大きく分けて以下のように展開します。

> トピックの導入
>
> ▼
>
> 最初のリスニング（全体の内容を大まかにつかむ）
>
> ▼
>
> 細部の確認（クイック・レスポンス、リテンション、リプロダクション＆インタープリテーション、ディクテーションといった通訳訓練法を活用して文章の細部を理解する）
>
> ▼
>
> リスニング（細部の確認後、全体を聴いて内容を理解する）
>
> ▼
>
> リーディング（リスニングで聴き取れなかった部分を読んで内容を確実に理解する）

本書では、これらのリスニングの活動を行う際に、ペアワークやグループワークを多く採り入れ、学習者同士がインタラクティブに学ぶことができるよう、また、受け身になりがちなリスニングの練習に対して能動的に取り組めるよう工夫をしています。

●ユニットの構成と効果的な学習法

Warm-up

ユニットで扱うトピックに関連する問題です。

1 イラストや写真を見てペアで話し合ってみましょう。

2 ペアやグループで話し合ってみましょう。

 はペアワークを

 はグループワークを表しています。

First Listening

最初のリスニングです。

3 パッセージ全体を聴いて、キャッチできた重要な語句を書き留めていきましょう。

4 書き取った語句をペアで確認してみましょう。

6

/// Vocabulary

ユニットのパッセージに使われている語彙の意味を確認します。クイック・レスポンスに挑戦してみましょう。クイック・レスポンスとは通訳訓練法の一つで、語彙を即座に訳出する練習です。

5 次の2種類の出題形式が用意されています。

奇数ユニット：まずリストに辞書を使って英語と日本語の訳語を入れます。その後にペアの一人が英語の語句を読み上げ、もう一人が即座に日本語に直し、その逆も行います。〈英→日〉、〈日→英〉と口頭でスピーディに直す練習を行いましょう。

偶数ユニット：リストに英語の語句とその意味が日本語で記載されています。ペアの一人が教科書を閉じ、もう一人がリスト内の語句を選んで英語で説明します。その際、該当する語句自体とその日本語訳を使ってはいけません。パートナーが正しい語句を言い当てられたら交替してください。

/// Retention / Reproduction and Interpretation

リテンションとリプロダクションの練習を行います。リテンションおよびリプロダクションとは、一定の長さの英文を一時的に記憶にとどめ、口頭で正確に再生する練習方法です。呼び方は通訳機関や書籍により異なることがありますが、本書では次のように定義しています。

- **リテンション**：1文（センテンス）を聴いた直後に口頭で再現すること。
- **リプロダクション**：長い文を意味のかたまりで切って再現していくこと。なお、このリプロダクションを行った後に、日本語で訳出していくことがインタープリテーション（通訳）です。

このアクティビティも奇数・偶数ユニットによって異なる出題形式が用意されています。ペアで練習をしましょう。それぞれ指定されているページを開きましょう。

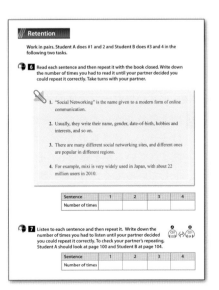

奇数ユニット：リテンションの練習です。

6 1〜4の各センテンスでは、まず目で読んで記憶に保持する練習をします。何度も後ろに戻って読むことはせずに、左から右へ一度だけ目で読んで覚えこみ、再生してください。

7 1〜4の各センテンスを聴いて記憶し、再生する練習をします。音声は3回流れます。

偶数ユニット：リプロダクションとインタープリテーションの練習です。

6 意味を持った単語のかたまりを聴いて繰り返す練習をします。

7 もう一度同じ音声を聴いて、それを日本語に訳していく練習をします。

Dictation

音声を聴いて、正確に文字に書き起こす練習です。

8 抜けている単語とその場所も正確に聴き取る必要があります。

9 ペアで答え合わせをしましょう。

Dictation (panel)

8 Several words are missing in the following paragraph. Listen to the CD and identify where. Make a slash (/) where a word is missing and write the missing word below the slash. The first answer is done for you.

"Social Networking" is the name given to a / form of online

ex. modern

communication. Most, users create a "profile," and on their profile the

users put about themselves. Usually, they write their name, date-of-birth,

hobbies and interests, and so on. Members can also photos, tell people

how they are feeling and what they are doing, and on other people's pages.

There are many different social networking sites, and different ones are

popular in different. For example, mixi is very widely used in Japan, with

about 22 million users in 2010. In 2011, the social networking site was

Facebook, which had more than 750 million active users and was

translated into over 100 languages.

9 Compare with a partner and see if you have the same answers.

Listening and Summarizing

リテンションなどの練習で細部を確認した後、再度リスニングを行います。パッセージ全体を聴き、内容を理解しましょう。

10 出題されている内容を正確にとらえましょう。メモを取る練習もしましょう。

11 もう一度同じ音声を聴いて、全体の内容を自分の言葉でまとめる練習をしてみましょう。英語でも日本語でも構いません。

Listening and Summarizing (panel)

10 Listen to the CD. Write down the pros and cons of social networking. Share with your partner what you have written down.

Pros	Cons

11 Listen again. Summarize what you have heard (either in Japanese or in English). Share your summary with your partner.

Post-Listening

最後に必ずパッセージ全体のスクリプトを読みましょう。

12 聴き取れなかった部分をそのままに放置しておいてはいけません。聴き取れなかった部分はどのように発音して読まれているかを確認し、それを自分の頭の中にインプットしていってください。"聴く"と"読む"を何度も繰り返し、耳と目で理解をつなげていきます。各パッセージは 400 語前後の文章です。50 語ごとにマークしていますので速読の練習にも使えます。

Post-Listening (panel)

12 Read the entire passage. Compare it with what you understood when you listened to it for the first time in **3** at the First Listening.

The Rise of Social Networking

"Social Networking" is the name given to a modern form of online communication. Most simply, users create a "profile," and on their profile the users put details about themselves. Usually, they write their name, gender, date-of-birth, hobbies and interests, and so on. Members can also upload photos, tell people how they are feeling and what they are doing, and comment on other people's pages. There are many different social networking sites, and different ones are popular in different regions. For example, mixi is very widely used in Japan, with about 22 million users in 2010. In 2011, the biggest social networking site was Facebook, which had more than 750 million active users and was translated into over 100 languages.

Social networking began as a way to meet and stay in contact with friends, and this is still true. However, other uses have been found. For example, sites like LinkedIn help people make professional contacts to search for jobs. Advertisers have also seen the possibility to reach millions of people easily (it is estimated that Facebook made over $1.8 billion from advertising in 2010). Data from social networking sites is increasingly used in criminal trials, teachers use the sites as a convenient way to communicate with students and students' parents, and many parties, large gatherings, and even mass demonstrations are organized through social networking sites. Clearly, the ability to easily share so much information has a wide range of possible uses.

However, there are risks. Many people put too much personal information onto these sites, and this information could be used against them by their employer, large corporations, or even governments. Privacy is actually a big problem; there is a concern, for example, that sexual predators* can use online data to get close to other users. One great fear, especially for parents, is that of "cyber-bullying," or online bullying. Sadly, there have been cases of teenagers committing suicide after being bullied through social networking sites. As sites like Facebook grow bigger and bigger, these concerns should certainly be carefully considered.

Social networking is an extremely valuable modern concept, and it continues to grow. If the risks mentioned above are controlled in the correct way, it is quite possible that social networking will be a great benefit for humankind.

*sexual predators: 性犯罪者
(377 words)

Society

The Rise of Social Networking

Warm-up

1 Look at this picture. Discuss the question below with a partner.

What do you think the two people are doing?

2 Work in groups of 4. Discuss the following questions.

a. Which of the following are social networking sites? Circle the correct ones.

mixi   Google   Yahoo   Facebook   LinkedIn   Myspace

b. Ask members in your group if they belong to any social networking sites.

Name	Are you a member of any social networking sites?	Which ones?	How often do you check them?
ex. Yoko	Yes	mixi	Twice a day

First Listening

3 Listen to the CD once. Write down any key words you hear.

CD1
02

4 Discuss what you were able to catch with your partner.

Vocabulary

5 Work in pairs. First, use a dictionary and complete the chart below by yourself. Then, check the answers with your partner. Put a check (✔) in the box if you answered correctly.

English	Japanese	✔
detail		
stay in contact		
criminal trial		
concern		
valuable		

Japanese	English	✔
広告主		
雇用主		
政府		
いじめ		
自殺する		

10

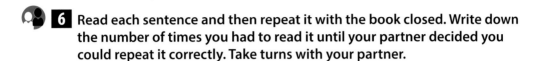

Retention

Work in pairs. Student A does #1 and 2 and Student B does #3 and 4 in the following two tasks.

6 Read each sentence and then repeat it with the book closed. Write down the number of times you had to read it until your partner decided you could repeat it correctly. Take turns with your partner.

> 1. "Social Networking" is the name given to a modern form of online communication.
>
> 2. Usually, they write their name, gender, date-of-birth, hobbies and interests, and so on.
>
> 3. There are many different social networking sites, and different ones are popular in different regions.
>
> 4. For example, mixi is very widely used in Japan, with about 22 million users in 2010.

Sentence	1	2	3	4
Number of times				

7 Listen to each sentence and then repeat it. Write down the number of times you had to listen until your partner decided you could repeat it correctly. To check your partner's repeating, Student A should look at page 100 and Student B at page 104.

Sentence	1	2	3	4
Number of times				

Dictation

8 Several words are missing in the following paragraph. Listen to the CD and identify where. Make a slash (/) where a word is missing and write the missing word below the slash. The first answer is done for you.

"Social Networking" is the name given to a / form of online

ex. modern

communication. Most, users create a "profile," and on their profile the

users put about themselves. Usually, they write their name, date-of-birth,

hobbies and interests, and so on. Members can also photos, tell people

how they are feeling and what they are doing, and on other people's pages.

There are many different social networking sites, and different ones are

popular in different. For example, mixi is very widely used in Japan, with

about 22 million users in 2010. In 2011, the social networking site was

Facebook, which had more than 750 million active users and was

translated into over 100 languages.

9 Compare with a partner and see if you have the same answers.

Listening and Summarizing

10 Listen to the CD. Write down the pros and cons of social networking. Share with your partner what you have written down.

Pros	Cons

11 Listen again. Summarize what you have heard (either in Japanese or in English). Share your summary with your partner.

12 Read the entire passage. Compare it with what you understood when you listened to it for the first time in **3** at the First Listening.

The Rise of Social Networking

"Social Networking" is the name given to a modern form of online communication. Most simply, users create a "profile," and on their profile the users put details about themselves. Usually, they write their name, gender, date-of-birth, hobbies and interests, and so on. Members can also upload photos, tell people how they are feeling and what they are doing, and comment
5 on other people's pages. There are many different social networking sites, and different ones are popular in different regions. For example, mixi is very widely used in Japan, with about 22 million users in 2010. In 2011, the biggest social networking site was Facebook, which had more than 750 million active users and was translated into over 100 languages.

Social networking began as a way to meet and stay in contact with friends, and this is still
10 true. However, other uses have been found. For example, sites like LinkedIn help people make professional contacts to search for jobs. Advertisers have also seen the possibility to reach millions of people easily (it is estimated that Facebook made over $1.8 billion from advertising in 2010). Data from social networking sites is increasingly used in criminal trials, teachers use the sites as a convenient way to communicate with students and students' parents, and many parties,
15 large gatherings, and even mass demonstrations are organized through social networking sites. Clearly, the ability to easily share so much information has a wide range of possible uses.

However, there are risks. Many people put too much personal information onto these sites, and this information could be used against them by their employer, large corporations, or even governments. Privacy is actually a big problem; there is a concern, for example, that sexual
20 predators* can use online data to get close to other users. One great fear, especially for parents, is that of "cyber-bullying," or online bullying. Sadly, there have been cases of teenagers committing suicide after being bullied through social networking sites. As sites like Facebook grow bigger and bigger, these concerns should certainly be carefully considered.

Social networking is an extremely valuable modern concept, and it continues to grow. If the risks
25 mentioned above are controlled in the correct way, it is quite possible that social networking will be a great benefit for humankind.

*sexual predators: 性犯罪者

(377 words)

The FIFA Football World Cup

 1 **Look at this picture. Discuss the questions below with a partner.**

 Do you know which country these football shirts belong to?

Can you guess what the stars on the shirt mean?

2 **Work in groups of 4. Discuss the following questions.**

a. Which of the following are football players? Circle the correct ones.

Rafael Nadal	Michael Jordan	Christiano Ronaldo
Tiger Woods	Lionel Messi	David Beckham

b. When do you think the following sporting events began? Rank them (earliest = 1):

Rank	Sporting Event	Rank	Sporting Event
	The Football World Cup		The modern Olympics
	The Super Bowl (American football)		The Rugby World Cup
	The Olympics		The Cricket World Cup
	Wimbledon (tennis)		The World Series (baseball)

3 Listen to the CD once. Write down any key words you hear.

CD1 07

4 Discuss what you were able to catch with your partner.

Vocabulary

5 Work in pairs. When your partner has closed the textbook, choose a word from the list below and explain the word to your partner. Do not say the word itself or the Japanese translation. When your partner has guessed the word, switch roles. Put a check (✔) if you can give the correct word.

Words	日本語の意味	✔
aftermath	余波・影響	
competition	競技	
current	現在の	
controversy	論争	
disaster	大惨事	
Minister	大臣	
extremely	極めて	
tragic	悲惨な	
get behind	応援する	
spectacle	光景・見世物	

Reproduction and Interpretation

Work in pairs. Switch with your partner when one of you has finished the following two tasks.

6 Listen to the CD. First, Student A repeats the first part after the beep, and then Student B repeats the second part. To check your partner's repeating, Student A should look at page 100 and Student B at page 104.

7 Listen to the CD again. This time, interpret the phrases after the beep into Japanese. Check with your partner.

Dictation

8 Several words are missing in the following paragraph. Listen to the CD and identify where. Make a slash (/) where a word is missing and write the missing word below the slash. The first answer is done for you.

In the competition's / format, 32 teams participate in the World Cup

ex. current

"finals," after qualifying from one of six regions. For the in 2010, a total

of 204 teams to qualify. Brazil is the only team to have qualified for and

participated in every World Cup since the began. In fact, Brazil is the most

successful team in the of the competition, having the trophy an impressive

five times. Actually, the trophy has only ever been by eight teams: Brazil,

Italy, (West) Germany, Argentina, England, France, and Spain.

9 Compare with a partner and see if you have the same answers.

Listening and Summarizing

10 Listen to the CD. Write down what happened involving the following countries. Share with your partner what you have written down.

Country	Incident
Argentina	
France	
Ireland	
El Salvador	
Columbia	

11 Listen again. Summarize what you have heard (either in Japanese or in English). Share your summary with your partner.

12 Read the entire passage. Compare it with what you understood when you listened to it for the first time in **3** at the First Listening.

The FIFA Football World Cup

The FIFA World Cup is one of the most important global sporting events. The first World Cup took place in 1930, and with the exception of 1942 and 1946—cancelled due to World War II and its aftermath—the World Cup has been held every four years since. Today, it is one of the most watched sporting events on the planet, with more than a billion people tuning in to see at least
5   some part of the 2010 final between Spain and the Netherlands.

In the competition's current format, 32 teams participate in the World Cup "finals," after first qualifying from one of six regions. For the tournament in 2010, a total of 204 teams attempted to qualify. Brazil is the only team to have qualified for and participated in every World Cup since the event began. In fact, Brazil is the most successful team in the history of the competition,
10   having lifted the trophy an impressive five times. Actually, the trophy has only ever been won by eight teams: Brazil, Italy, (West) Germany, Argentina, Uruguay, England, France, and Spain.

With so much at stake on, potentially, one kick of a ball, it is inevitable that controversy and even disaster will ensue. Everybody remembers Maradona's "Hand of God," for example. A similar handball incident occurred in the 2009 qualifying stages, in which France's Thierry Henry
15   handled the ball against Ireland. This actually led Ireland's Justice Minister to publicly demand a replay. Unbelievably, in 1969, a World Cup qualifying match between Central American countries El Salvador and Honduras is thought to have been partly responsible for war breaking out between the two nations. One of the most tragic episodes in the history of the competition is the fate of Andrés Escobar, the Columbian player murdered in 1994 after scoring an own goal
20   that sent his team out of the tournament.

Despite these incidents, the World Cup remains an extremely important event in the sporting calendar. It provides an opportunity for the world's best to display their skills to a global audience, and it allows the host nation to show off the country to a huge influx of foreign media and supporters. It also helps to bring the game of football to more and more people worldwide.
25   Most importantly, the World Cup is a chance for fans around the world to get behind their team and enjoy a magnificent month-long spectacle.

(399 words)

"Cool Japan"

Warm-up

1 Look at this picture. Discuss the questions below with a partner.

Have you heard of the expression "Cool Japan"?

What things come to mind when you hear the expression "Cool Japan"?

2 Work in groups of 4. Discuss the following question.

Ask members in your group which anime, manga, or video games they like and ask them to explain those briefly.

Name	Favorite anime, manga, or video games	Brief explanation
ex. Naoki	Anime and manga called "Captain Tsubasa"	• Known as "Flash Kicker" • Story about a Japanese youth soccer team and the team captain Tsubasa

3 Listen to the CD once. Write down any key words you hear.

CD1
12

4 Discuss what you were able to catch with your partner.

5 Work in pairs. First, use a dictionary and complete the chart below by yourself. Then, check the answers with your partner. Put a check (✔) in the box if you answered correctly.

English	Japanese	✔
capture		
economic downturn		
in recent years		
accessible		
overcome		
Japanese	**English**	✔
経済産業省		
利益、恩恵		
著しく		
およそ		
高齢化する人口		

Retention

Work in pairs. Student A does #1 and 2 and Student B does #3 and 4 in the following two tasks.

 6 Read each sentence and then repeat it with the book closed. Write down the number of times you had to read it until your partner decided you could repeat it correctly. Take turns with your partner.

1. Nowadays other parts of Japanese culture capture people's imagination and excitement around the world.

2. The Japanese government is now trying more and more to have global influence through "soft power."

3. With soft power, you gain influence by creating a positive and sympathetic image of your own country.

4. The global image of Japan will improve, helping the country economically and politically.

Sentence	1	2	3	4
Number of times				

7 Listen to each sentence and then repeat it. Write down the number of times you had to listen until your partner decided you could repeat it correctly. To check your partner's repeating, Student A should look at page 100 and Student B at page 104.

Sentence	1	2	3	4
Number of times				

Dictation

8 Several words are missing in the following paragraph. Listen to the CD and identify where. Make a slash (/) where a word is missing and write the missing word below the slash. The first answer is done for you.

Traditionally, when / people thought of Japan, they might have the land

       ex. non-Japanese

of kabuki theater, haiku poetry, and sumo wrestling. Although these are

still strongly with Japan, nowadays other parts of Japanese culture capture

people's imagination and around the world. Instead of sushi and samurai,

Japan is now often thought of as the country of video games, manga, and

cosplay.

This may not be a bad thing. Since the of the Second World War and the

economic downturn of the, Japan's "hard power" (the ability to forcibly

influence other countries) has been. Instead, the Japanese government is

now trying more and more to have global through "soft power."

---

 9 Compare with a partner and see if you have the same answers.

Listening and Summarizing

10 Listen to the CD. Answer the following questions. Share with your partner what you have written down.

1. There are two major benefits expected thanks to Japan's "cultural industries." What are they?

In the short term	In the medium and long term

2. What have been the successes of Japan's "soft power"?

3. What does the writer believe this kind of accessible culture will bring to Japan?

11 Listen again. Summarize what you have heard (either in Japanese or in English). Share your summary with your partner.

12 Read the entire passage. Compare it with what you understood when you listened to it for the first time in **3** at the First Listening.

"Cool Japan"

Traditionally, when non-Japanese people thought of Japan, they might have pictured the land of kabuki theater, haiku poetry, and sumo wrestling. Although these are still strongly linked with Japan, nowadays other parts of Japanese culture capture people's imagination and excitement around the world. Instead of sushi and samurai, Japan is now often thought of as the country of
5 video games, manga, anime, and cosplay.

This may not be a bad thing. Since the end of the Second World War and the economic downturn of the 1990s, Japan's "hard power" (the ability to forcibly influence other countries) has been decreasing. Instead, the Japanese government is now trying more and more to have global influence through "soft power." With soft power, you gain influence by creating a positive and
10 sympathetic image of your own country, making other countries want to cooperate with you. Therefore, the Ministry of Economy, Trade and Industry (METI) is now aiming to promote Japanese "cultural industries" (manga, fashion, and suchlike) throughout the world. The hope is that there will be two major benefits: in the short term, the Japanese economy will profit from increased sales and tourism; in the medium and long term, the global image of Japan will
15 improve, helping the country economically and politically.

This government policy, informally known as "Cool Japan," may already be having some success. For example, an annual fashion show in Tokyo, called "Tokyo Girls Collection," attracts many young girls from overseas. Also, when travelling outside of Japan it is very common to see Hello Kitty dolls, manga comics, Japanese movies, and so on. More significantly, the number
20 of foreign students studying in Japan has increased sharply in recent years, and is now fast approaching 100,000. Approximately 90% of these students are from Asian countries, where older generations might have negative feelings towards Japan (due to the events of World War II). This suggests that such feelings are not as strongly felt among today's younger generation, and it may in part be thanks to the idea of "Cool Japan" taking hold.

25 "Cool Japan" alone will not solve Japan's deeper economic problems, such as the aging population and the decreasing birthrate. However, the more the world feels that Japan is a modern, exciting, accessible culture, the more Japan has the chance of obtaining global support in overcoming its difficulties.

(386 words)

From Rags to Riches: A Story of J.K. Rowling

Warm-up

 1 Look at this picture. Discuss the question below with a partner.

 Do you know the people in the picture? Who do you think they are?

 2 Work in groups of 4. Discuss the following questions.

a. Ask members in your group if they have read any books or watched any movies of the *Harry Potter* series.

b. Ask members in your group who they like best in the *Harry Potter* series and why.

Name	The character they like most	Reason
ex. Mariko	Ron Weasley	Ron always stands by his friends.

3 Listen to the CD once. Write down any key words you hear.

CD1 17

4 Discuss what you were able to catch with your partner.

Vocabulary

5 Work in pairs. When your partner has closed the textbook, choose a word from the list below and explain the word to your partner. Do not say the word itself or the Japanese translation. When your partner has guessed the word, switch roles. Put a check (✔) if you can give the correct word.

Words	日本語の意味	✔
state benefit	公的給付金	
old-fashioned	古めかしい	
go by ~	~の名前で通す	
mirror	反映する	
secondary education	中等教育	
be credited with ~	~で高い評価を得る	
household name	誰でもよく知っている名前	
runner-up	2位	
rags-to-riches story	立身出世物語（無一文から大金持ちになった話）	
inspiration	鼓舞するもの	

Reproduction and Interpretation

Work in pairs. Switch with your partner when one of you has finished the following two tasks.

6 Listen to the CD. First, Student A repeats the first part after the beep, and then Student B repeats the second part. To check your partner's repeating, Student A should look at page 100 and Student B at page 104.

7 Listen to the CD again. This time, interpret the phrases after the beep into Japanese. Check with your partner.

Dictation

8 Several words are missing in the following paragraph. Listen to the CD and identify where. Make a slash (/) where a word is missing and write the missing word below the slash. The first answer is done for you.

The book was published in June 1997, and was / by six more (a total of

<u>ex. followed</u>

seven *Harry Potter* books, the seven years of secondary education in the

U.K.). In total, the books have now sold more than copies, and have been

translated into about languages. They are credited with children to read

more at a time when video games, television, and the Internet are more

and more. The books were also into a hugely successful movie franchise,

over which Rowling maintained control. In particular, she insisted that had

to be British, filming of the movies had to be in Britain, and she also had

to to the movie scripts before filming began.

 9 Compare with a partner and see if you have the same answers.

Listening and Summarizing

10 Listen to the CD. Answer the following questions. Share with your partner what you have written down.

1. What are the two pieces of advice that a publishing company gave J.K. Rowling?

First piece of advice	
Second piece of advice	

2. Write down what J.K. Rowling's life was like before and after the success of the *Harry Potter* books.

Before publishing	
After publishing	

11 Listen again. Summarize what you have heard (either in Japanese or in English). Share your summary with your partner.

12 Read the entire passage. Compare it with what you understood when you listened to it for the first time in **3** at the First Listening.

From Rags to Riches: A Story of J.K. Rowling

Joanne Rowling was born in Gloucestershire, England, in 1965. In 1995, she was a single mother living in Edinburgh, Scotland, relying on state benefits to feed herself and her young daughter. At that time, she was writing a book based on an idea she had had five years earlier, in 1990, while sitting on a train. Most of the writing was done in cafés in Edinburgh, simply because it was
5 easier for her to get her baby to sleep when they were out of the small apartment they were living in. While her daughter was sleeping, Joanne was able to write.

The book was finished in 1995. The title was *Harry Potter and the Philosopher's Stone*, and it was typed on an old-fashioned typewriter. The manuscript was sent to 12 publishing companies, all of which said "no." Finally, in 1996 a company called Bloomsbury said "yes." Rowling was
10 given two pieces of advice. Firstly, she should go by the pen-name of J.K. Rowling, instead of Joanne, because young boys might not want to read a book written by a woman. She didn't have a middle name, so she just inserted the "K." Secondly, she should get another job, because she would not make much money from this book.

The book was published in June 1997, and was followed by six more (a total of seven *Harry*
15 *Potter* books, mirroring the seven years of secondary education in the U.K.). In total, the books have now sold more than 450 million copies, and have been translated into about 70 languages. They are credited with encouraging children to read more at a time when video games, television, and the Internet are more and more widespread. The books were also adapted into a hugely successful movie franchise, over which Rowling maintained considerable control. In particular,
20 she insisted that actors had to be British, filming of the movies had to be in Britain, and she also had to agree to the movie scripts before filming began.

Today, J.K. Rowling is a household name. In 2008 she was named as the 12th richest woman in Britain, and she was the runner-up in the Time Person of the Year award in 2007. Could she have dreamed of such success back in 1995 while sitting in a café, or even in 1990 while sitting on a
25 train? This rags-to-riches story should be an inspiration to us all.

(399 words)

Studying Abroad for Japanese University Students

 Warm-up

 1 Look at this picture. Discuss the question below with a partner.

What do you think these students are doing?

 2 Work in groups of 4. Discuss the following questions.

a. About how many Japanese students are studying at universities in the U.S.? Circle the correct answer.

| 10,000 | 26,000 | 58,000 | 75,000 | 300,000 |

b. Ask members in your group if they are interested in studying overseas. If they answer yes, ask how long and where they want to go. If they answer no, ask why not.

Name	Would you like to study overseas?	If yes, how long and where?	If no, why not?
ex. Toshiki	Yes	He wants to attend a summer program at University of Hawaii for one month.	

First Listening

3 Listen to the CD once. Write down any key words you hear.

CD1 22

4 Discuss what you were able to catch with your partner.

Vocabulary

5 Work in pairs. First, use a dictionary and complete the chart below by yourself. Then, check the answers with your partner. Put a check (✔) in the box if you answered correctly.

English	Japanese	✔
introverted		
indifferent		
quota		
disturbing		
industrialist		
Japanese	**English**	✔
報道		
強固にする		
5年連続		
一応は		
記者会見		

Retention

Work in pairs. Student A does #1 and 2 and Student B does #3 and 4 in the following two tasks.

 6 Read each sentence and then repeat it with the book closed. Write down the number of times you had to read it until your partner decided you could repeat it correctly. Take turns with your partner.

1. Some provide financial support and some give English courses to prepare students for living overseas.

2. Experiencing diversity and meeting people from different cultures is a worthy challenge for today's youth.

3. They claim that the tendency is due to problems such as finance.

4. It is the youth of today who will determine whether Japan is to become a true presence in the international community.

Sentence	1	2	3	4
Number of times				

 7 Listen to each sentence and then repeat it. Write down the number of times you had to listen until your partner decided you could repeat it correctly. To check your partner's repeating, Student A should look at page 101 and Student B at page 105.

Sentence	1	2	3	4
Number of times				

 **Dictation**

8 Several words are missing in the following paragraph. Listen to the CD and identify where. Make a slash (/) where a word is missing and write the missing word below the slash. The first answer is done for you.

To reinforce this / , data published by the Institute of International
        ex. criticism

Education in the U.S. has often been to. According to the data, the number

of Japanese students studying in the U.S. has been for five consecutive

years, while numbers from China, India, and South Korea have all been

increasing. There are 127,000 Chinese students, Indian students, and

South Korean students in the U.S., but only 26,000 Japanese students.

These figures are disturbing, especially in of the fact that

internationalization has supposedly been in Japan.

 9 Compare with a partner and see if you have the same answers.

Listening and Summarizing

10 Listen to the CD. Write down the details and remarks of the two people from academia and industry, and the possible consequences of young people's actions.

CD1 26

	Academic	Industrialist
Name		
Career		
Remarks		

Possible consequences

11 Listen again. Summarize what you have heard (either in Japanese or in English). Share with your partner.

CD1 26

Post-Listening

12 Read the entire passage. Compare it with what you understood when you listened to it for the first time in **3** at the First Listening.

Studying Abroad for Japanese University Students

The tendency of Japanese youngsters to be somewhat introverted has been frequently mentioned in recent media coverage. Young people are said to be indifferent to anything outside of Japan. In some universities, the number of students who attend summer or spring programs abroad, as well as longer one-year programs, has not reached the designated quota. This inclination leads
5 older generations to fear that Japan may become isolated from the world or left behind in the international community.

To reinforce this criticism, data published by the Institute of International Education in the U.S. has often been referred to. According to the data, the number of Japanese students studying in the U.S. has been decreasing for five consecutive years, while numbers from China, India, and
10 South Korea have all been steadily increasing. There are currently 127,000 Chinese students, 105,000 Indian students, and 72,000 South Korean students in the U.S., but only 26,000 Japanese students. These figures are disturbing, especially in light of the fact that internationalization has supposedly been promoted in Japan.

In fact, worried about the future of this country, Eiichi Negishi, in a 2010 press conference after
15 winning the Nobel Prize in chemistry, called for Japanese people to go overseas and try "knight errantry."* This was based on his own experiences. Such sentiments have been voiced not only by academics but also by industrialists, such as Tadashi Yanai, CEO of UNIQLO, who has appealed to youngsters to go overseas and expand their horizons. Many universities also encourage students, and try different ways to aid them to go abroad. Some provide financial
20 support and some give English courses to prepare students for living overseas. The belief is that experiencing diversity and meeting people from different cultures is a worthy challenge for today's youth, a challenge that will provide experience and character in their later lives.

Some people argue that the trend outlined above is simply not true, or they claim that the tendency is due to problems such as finance, not the insular nature of young Japanese people.
25 However, one thing is for sure: the future of this country falls on young people's shoulders. It is the youth of today who will determine whether Japan is to become a true presence in the international community, or if it will just be another Galapagos—isolated and frozen in time.

* 武者修行

(387 words)

Stress in Modern Society

Warm-up

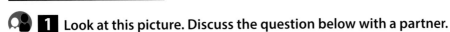 **1** Look at this picture. Discuss the question below with a partner.

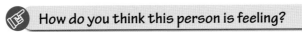 How do you think this person is feeling?

2 Discuss the following questions:

a. Work in pairs. When do you feel stressed?

b. Work in groups of 4. Ask members in your group how they cope with stress.

Name	How to cope with stress
ex. Eriko	She goes to a dessert buffet and eat sweets.

First Listening

3 Listen to the CD once. Write down any key words you hear.

CD1 27

Vocabulary

5 Work in pairs. When your partner has closed the textbook, choose a word from the list below and explain the word to your partner. Do not say the word itself or the Japanese translation. When your partner has guessed the word, switch roles. Put a check (✔) if you can give the correct word.

Words	日本語の意味	✔
impact	衝撃	
nervous	緊張して	
anxiety	不安	
vicious circle	悪循環	
avoid	避ける	
damaging	有害な	
competitive	競争の激しい	
off-key	音程のはずれた	
cope with	対処する	
regret	後悔する	

4 Discuss what you were able to catch with your partner.

Reproduction and Interpretation

Work in pairs. Switch with your partner when one of you has finished the following two tasks.

6 Listen to the CD. First, Student A repeats the first part after the beep, and then Student B repeats the second part. To check your partner's repeating, Student A should look at page 101 and Student B at page 105.

7 Listen to the CD again. This time, interpret the phrases after the beep into Japanese. Check with your partner.

Dictation

8 Several words are missing in the following paragraph. Listen to the CD and identify where. Make a slash (/) where a word is missing and write the missing word below the slash. The first answer is done for you.

Stress is actually a / feeling of worry or anxiety that a person from
ex. non-stop

relaxing. It is not something that for a few moments and then magically

disappears; it is. Everybody's reaction to stress is different. People who

suffer from stress might a lot of weight, or they might lose a lot of weight.

They might find it very difficult to sleep, which makes them, which makes

them more stressed, which makes it even more difficult to sleep. This is

called a "vicious circle." They might get a headache, or, or backache.

Maybe they will get with other people very quickly. In short, the of stress

can be negative, and can make a person's life very difficult. Stress can

even a person's life away.

 9 Compare with a partner and see if you have the same answers.

Listening and Summarizing

10 Listen to the CD. Write down examples of ways to relax. Then write how different people react to these examples.

Example	For some people	For other people

11 Listen again. Summarize what you have heard (either in Japanese or in English). Share your summary with your partner.

12 Read the entire passage. Compare it with what you understood when you listened to it for the first time in **3** at the First Listening.

Stress in Modern Society

Stress. This is a word that has become very common in the modern world. You can often hear people say things like "I'm so stressed today," or "That was a stressful conversation." In fact, the word has become so common in the English language that it no longer has the same impact as it did before. These days, the word "stress" is more often used as another way to say we are busy,
5 or nervous, or just uncomfortable. That's OK; languages change, and the meanings of words also change. However, we should not forget the original meaning of the word "stress," because what it creates is a serious problem, and the fast pace of the modern world continues to make it more and more serious.

Stress is actually a non-stop feeling of worry or anxiety that prevents a person from relaxing.
10 It is not something that lasts for a few moments and then magically disappears; it is constant. Everybody's reaction to stress is different. People who suffer from stress might gain a lot of weight, or they might lose a lot of weight. They might find it very difficult to sleep, which makes them tired, which makes them more stressed, which makes it even more difficult to sleep. This is called a "vicious circle." They might get a headache, or stomachache, or backache. Maybe they
15 will get angry with other people very quickly. In short, the effects of stress can be negative, and can make a person's life very difficult. Stress can even take a person's life away.

So, if you want to avoid the damaging effects of stress, what can you do? That's not an easy question to answer, because everyone is different. What you must do is find what works for you, in order to relax. For example, some people find that sport and exercise are great ways to become
20 healthy, while lowering stress at the same time. But other people hate the competitive nature of sport, and find that playing it makes them more stressed. Other people love going to karaoke, and find that shouting into a microphone in their loudest voice makes them feel great. Other people, however, believe that listening to their friends sing bad songs, badly off-key, is extremely stressful.

25 There is no easy answer, because not everybody is the same. But what is certain is that in modern society you need to find your own way to cope with stress. If you don't, you might regret it.

(414 words)

Bankers' Bonuses: A Moral Issue

Warm-up

1 Look at this picture. Discuss the questions below with a partner.

👉 Have you heard of the term "sub-prime loan"?

👉 When and where did this crisis occur?

2 Work in groups of 4. Discuss the following questions.

a. Which of the following are financial institutions? Circle the correct ones.

HSBC   H&M   Citibank   Goldman Sachs   Fast Retailing

b. Discuss which cities have the following financial districts.

Financial district	City
Kabuto cho	
The City	
Central	
Wall Street	
Raffles Place	
Kitahama	

First Listening

3 Listen to the CD once. Write down any key words you hear.

CD1
32

4 Discuss what you were able to catch with your partner.

Vocabulary

5 Work in pairs. First, use a dictionary and complete the chart below by yourself. Then, check the answers with your partner. Put a check (✔) in the box if you answered correctly.

English	Japanese	✔
reckless		
go bankrupt		
bail out		
outcry		
excess		
Japanese	**English**	**✔**
中堅の		
投資家		
金融業界		
保険会社		
補償		

Retention

Work in pairs. Student A does #1 and 2 and Student B does #3 and 4 in the following two tasks.

 6 Read each sentence and then repeat it with the book closed. Write down the number of times you had to read it until your partner decided you could repeat it correctly. Take turns with your partner.

1. Governments were very keen to make sure that large financial institutions did not go bankrupt.

2. In the U.S. alone, $245 billion was given to U.S. banks.

3. This was viewed by the general public as money straight from the regular taxpayer's pocket.

4. Public discontent turned to anger when people learned of the salary bonuses.

Sentence	1	2	3	4
Number of times				

 7 Listen to each sentence and then repeat it. Write down the number of times you had to listen until your partner decided you could repeat it correctly. To check your partner's repeating, Student A should look at page 101 and Student B at page 105.

Sentence	1	2	3	4
Number of times				

Dictation

8 Several words are missing in the following paragraph. Listen to the CD and identify where. Make a slash (/) where a word is missing and write the missing word below the slash. The first answer is done for you.

The sub-prime loan /̸ in the U.S., and the failure of a mid-sized bank in
ex. crisis

the U.K., were two of a number of major events that a crisis in 2008 that

threatened to some of the largest and most powerful banks and financial in

the world. It highlighted that certain banks and investors had become

reckless and, and hadn't fully considered the risks of their actions, nor

what might happen if the markets turned against them.

Governments were very to make sure that large financial institutions—

which were to the working of the economy—did not go bankrupt. They

decided to "bail out" certain banks and corporations that were at of going

under. This meant giving them sums of money—in the U.S. alone, $245

billion was given to U.S. banks.

 9 Compare with a partner and see if you have the same answers.

Listening and Summarizing

10 Listen to the CD. Write down about an infamous example of salary bonuses and the measure taken by the U.S. government to cope with the public outcry.

Infamous example	U.S. government's measure

11 Listen again. Summarize what you have heard (either in Japanese or in English). Share your summary with your partner.

12 Read the entire passage. Compare it with what you understood when you listened to it for the first time in **3** at the First Listening.

Bankers' Bonuses: A Moral Issue

The sub-prime loan crisis in the U.S., and the failure of a mid-sized bank in the U.K., were two of a number of major events that triggered a crisis in 2008 that threatened to bankrupt some of the largest and most powerful banks and financial institutions in the world. It highlighted that certain banks and investors had become reckless and greedy, and hadn't fully considered the risks of
5 their actions, nor planned what might happen if the markets turned against them.

Governments were very keen to make sure that large financial institutions—which were essential to the working of the economy—did not go bankrupt. They decided to "bail out" certain banks and corporations that were at risk of going under. This meant giving them huge sums of money—in the U.S. alone, $245 billion was given to U.S. banks. The money was mostly in the form of
10 repayable loans, but also some money that did not need to be paid back. This was viewed by the general public as money straight from the regular taxpayer's pocket. Although most people understood the need to save those key businesses, there was also widespread discontent at having to pay for someone else's mistakes. The reputation of all bankers was damaged, including the vast majority who had no responsibility for the crisis.

15 Public discontent turned to anger when people learned of the salary bonuses some workers in the financial industry were receiving, especially those in corporations that had been saved using public money. Perhaps the most infamous example was that of the American International Group (AIG). This insurance company had declared losses of more than $60 billion in just the last quarter of 2008, and it had received $170 billion in government bailout money. However, it was
20 declared in 2009 that bonuses for employees in the finance division of the company would total $218 million. This "reward for failure" was considered completely unacceptable.

The huge public outcry led governments to try to somehow regulate the payment of bonuses. In the U.S., for example, a law was passed allowing for taxes as high as 90% on some bonuses awarded to companies that had received government money. Such measures have popular appeal,
25 but they have also been criticized. In countries that operate a free market economy, reward based on performance is an essential part of compensation. The need is clearly to control the excesses—the huge numbers involved, and the "reward for failure" culture that has developed.

(412 words)

Education in Singapore

 1 Look at this picture. Discuss the question below with a partner.

 Where is Singapore located?

2 Discuss the following questions:

 a. Work in pairs. Which one is roughly equivalent to the area of Singapore? Circle the correct one.

> Hyogo Prefecture   Shikoku   Tokyo   Tokyo's 23 wards

 b. Work in groups of 4. Which countries have more than one official language?

Countries with a bilingual policy

First Listening

3 Listen to the CD once. Write down any key words you hear.

CD1
37

4 Discuss what you were able to catch with your partner.

Vocabulary

5 Work in pairs. When your partner has closed the textbook, choose a word from the list below and explain the word to your partner. Do not say the word itself or the Japanese translation. When your partner has guessed the word, switch roles. Put a check (✔) if you can give the correct word.

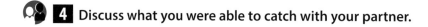

Words	日本語の意味	✔
academic qualification	学歴	
natural resource	天然資源	
principal	主要な	
knowledgeable	知識の豊富な	
mother tongue	母語	
enthusiastic	熱心な	
streaming	能力別学級編成	
MBA (Master of Business Administration)	経営学修士	
secure	確保する	
prosperous	繁栄した	

Reproduction and Interpretation

Work in pairs. Switch with your partner when one of you has finished the following two tasks.

6 Listen to the CD. First, Student A repeats the first part after the beep, and then Student B repeats the second part. To check your partner's repeating, Student A should look at page 101 and Student B at page 106.

7 Listen to the CD again. This time, interpret the phrases after the beep into Japanese. Check with your partner.

Dictation

8 Several words are missing in the following paragraph. Listen to the CD and identify where. Make a slash (/) where a word is missing and write the missing word below the slash. The first answer is done for you.

After secondary education, students can / pre-university education at a
                              ex. pursue

two-year junior college. Then, some will be able to enter one of the

universities in Singapore, although in ycars many have decided to study

overseas. Some students opt to go to one of five Polytechnics for more

practical study after secondary education. Many Singaporeans also to

study even after they get a job. There are many programs offered in

Singapore, such as an MBA (Master of Business Administration), which

people take to employment, get, or get a better job. Some people may feel

it is a society, but it is clear that those who have gone through the system

have helped a prosperous country with economic development.

 9 Compare with a partner and see if you have the same answers.

Listening and Summarizing

10 Listen to the CD. Write down details of the two key features of education in Singapore. [CD1 41]

Bilingual policy	Streaming system at an early stage

11 Listen again. Summarize what you have heard (either in Japanese or in English). Share your summary with your partner. [CD1 41]

12 Read the entire passage. Compare it with what you understood when you listened to it for the first time in **3** at the First Listening.

Education in Singapore

Singapore is a society that emphasizes academic qualifications. The government believes that since the country does not possess any natural resources, the population is the principal resource and must therefore be well-educated. Also, many Singaporeans believe that the more educated they are, the more chances they have to succeed in their careers. The result is a highly efficient
5 and effective education system that produces motivated and knowledgeable citizens.

One notable feature of the education in Singapore is the bilingual education policy. Although education is conducted in English, students also learn from an early age their mother tongue: either Malay, Chinese, or Tamil. Pupils' primary school education comprises two stages. In the first stage, Primary 1 to Primary 4, pupils are mainly taught English and their mother tongue
10 (about 60% of the curriculum), and mathematics (about 40%). Pupils are streamed into the second stage of primary education, Primary 5 and 6, based on their learning ability. In other words, their future academic course is determined by their early language and math skills. As you might expect, then, parents are extremely enthusiastic about the education of their children, and it is not unusual for young pupils to receive private tutoring.

15 In fact, the streaming system is another key feature of the education in Singapore. One of the biggest divisions takes place when pupils finish primary education. All pupils take a national exam called the Primary School Leaving Examination (PSLE) at the end of Primary 6. The results of the PSLE lead students to attend different courses of secondary education: Special, Express, and Normal courses. Students of Special and Express courses study four years, whereas
20 students of the Normal course (Academic) study five years in total to prepare for the next level.

After secondary education, students can pursue pre-university education at a two-year junior college. Then, some will be able to enter one of the universities in Singapore, although in recent years many have decided to study overseas instead. Some students opt to go to one of five Polytechnics for more practical study after secondary education. Many Singaporeans also
25 continue to study even after they get a job. There are many vocational programs offered in Singapore, such as an MBA (Master of Business Administration), which people take to secure employment, get promoted, or get a better job. Some people may feel it is a stressful society, but it is clear that those who have gone through the system have helped create a prosperous country with miraculous economic development.

(415 words)

Celebrities' Private Lives: Public Property?

 Warm-up

1 Look at this picture. Discuss the questions below with a partner.

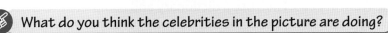
☞ **What do you think the celebrities in the picture are doing?**

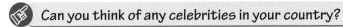
☞ **Can you think of any celebrities in your country?**

2 Work in groups of 4. Discuss the following questions.

a. Do you know the following celebrities? Why are they famous?

> Johnny Depp   Paris Hilton   Dewi Sukarno   Lady Gaga

b. Ask members in your group the pros and cons of disclosing celebrities' private lives.

Name	Pros	Cons
ex. Emi	It's entertaining to read about celebrities.	

First Listening

3 Listen to the CD once. Write down any key words you hear.

CD2
02

4 Discuss what you were able to catch with your partner.

Vocabulary

5 Work in pairs. First, use a dictionary and complete the chart below by yourself. Then, check the answers with your partner. Put a check (✔) in the box if you answered correctly.

English	Japanese	✔
award ceremony		
provoke		
reward		
exclusive		
half-decent		
Japanese	**English**	✔
出席する		
意図的に		
侵害		
近年、昨今		
攻撃的な、積極的な		

Retention

Work in pairs. Student A does #1 and 2 and Student B does #3 and 4 in the following two tasks.

 6 Read each sentence and then repeat it with the book closed. Write down the number of times you had to read it until your partner decided you could repeat it correctly. Take turns with your partner.

1. The driver lost control and the car crashed into the wall of a tunnel.

2. Many photographers who had been chasing the car simply took pictures of the crash.

3. Many people questioned whether the photographers had gone too far.

4. Celebrities expect to be photographed when they dress up and attend awards ceremonies and film premieres.

Sentence	1	2	3	4
Number of times				

7 Listen to each sentence and then repeat it. Write down the number of times you had to listen until your partner decided you could repeat it correctly. To check your partner's repeating, Student A should look at page 102 and Student B at page 106.

Sentence	1	2	3	4
Number of times				

8 Several words are missing in the following paragraph. Listen to the CD and identify where. Make a slash (/) where a word is missing and write the missing word below the slash. The first answer is done for you.

On August 31, 1997, Princess Diana and Dodi Al-Fayed were being driven

at / speeds through the streets of Paris. The driver, who had been, was

ex. dangerous

trying to get away from the photographers following them. The driver lost

and the car crashed into the of a tunnel. Three of the four people in the car

died, including Princess Diana. Many photographers who had been

chasing the car took pictures of the crash, and did not try to help. After

this, many people questioned whether the photographers had too far. Had

the paparazzi actually become "stalkerazzi?" The actress Elizabeth

Taylor—who spent her whole life in the spotlight—even called the people

who had been following Diana.

 9 Compare with a partner and see if you have the same answers.

Listening and Summarizing

10 Listen to the CD. Write down three reasons for invasion of private life. Share with your partner what you have written down.

First reason	Second reason	Third reason

11 Listen again. Summarize what you have heard (either in Japanese or in English). Share your summary with your partner.

12 Read the entire passage. Compare it with what you understood when you listened to it for the first time in **3** at the First Listening.

Celebrities' Private Lives: Public Property?

On August 31, 1997, Princess Diana and Dodi Al-Fayed were being driven at dangerous speeds through the streets of Paris. The driver, who had been drinking, was trying to get away from the photographers following them. The driver lost control and the car crashed into the wall of a tunnel. Three of the four people in the car died, including Princess Diana. Many photographers

5 who had been chasing the car simply took pictures of the crash, and did not try to help. After this accident, many people questioned whether the photographers had gone too far. Had the paparazzi actually become "stalkerazzi?" The actress Elizabeth Taylor—who spent her whole life in the media spotlight—even called the people who had been following Diana "murderers."

Celebrities have always been photographed, and in fact many celebrities *want* their pictures

10 taken—this creates publicity for them, and helps their careers. However, how far is too far? Of course, celebrities expect to be photographed when they dress up and attend awards ceremonies and film premieres. Is it OK, though, to take their picture when they are shopping? Or driving? Or just relaxing in their home? Is it OK to deliberately provoke a celebrity just so you can get a picture of them getting angry? Believe it or not, this does happen.

15 There seem to be three major reasons for this private life invasion. First, the reward for a "great" picture is very high. For example, the photo of Britney Spears having her head shaved is said to have been bought for $250,000 (about 30 million yen at the time). The result is the paparazzi will follow a celebrity anywhere just to get an exclusive picture. Second, anybody can take a picture. In recent years, the number of amateur paparazzi (somebody with a half-decent digital camera)

20 has increased greatly. Competition for good pictures is now fierce, and photographers need to be more aggressive to get the perfect photo they need. The third problem is the biggest: the public. We buy millions and millions of celebrity magazines, we watch entertainment TV, and we visit entertainment websites. We love seeing famous people, whether in a public or a private situation. We create the demand for these pictures, and if we continue, surely so will the paparazzi.

(379 words)

The Future of Energy

Warm-up

 1 Look at this picture. Discuss the question below with a partner.

How many of these do you think there are in Japan?
How many in the U.S.?

2 Work in groups of 4. Discuss the following question.

Which parts of the chart represent the following energy sources: hydraulic power, nuclear power, thermal power, others?

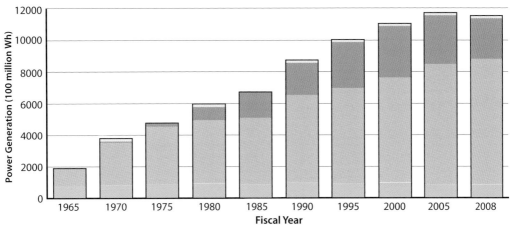

Energy Generated by Power Source in Japan
Data used: EDMC Handbook of Energy & Economic Statistics (2010)

First Listening

3 Listen to the CD once. Write down any key words you hear.

CD2
07

4 Discuss what you were able to catch with your partner.

Vocabulary

5 Work in pairs. When your partner has closed the textbook, choose a word from the list below and explain the word to your partner. Do not say the word itself or the Japanese translation. When your partner has guessed the word, switch roles. Put a check (✔) if you can give the correct word.

Words	日本語の意味	✔
devastating	壊滅的な	
consequences	結果	
nuclear power	原子力	
humanitarian	人道的	
as of ~	～現在で	
postpone	延期する	
fade	色あせる	
alternative	取って代わるもの	
renewable energy	再生可能エネルギー	
windmill	風車	

Reproduction and Interpretation

Work in pairs. Switch with your partner when one of you has finished the following two tasks.

6 Listen to the CD. First, Student A repeats the first part after the beep, and then Student B repeats the second part. To check your partner's repeating, Student A should look at page 102 and Student B at page 106.

7 Listen to the CD again. This time, interpret the phrases after the beep into Japanese. Check with your partner.

Dictation

8 Several words are missing in the following paragraph. Listen to the CD and identify where. Make a slash (/) where a word is missing and write the missing word below the slash. The first answer is done for you.

> What, though, are the / ? The demand for energy grows and grows, while
> **ex.** alternatives
>
> our of oil, coal, and natural gas will not forever. Perhaps the answer with
>
> renewable energy. In recent years, the use of renewable energy from
>
> natural such as the sun, wind, and oceans has become more and more
>
> widespread. Common examples of renewable energy are panels on the
>
> roof of houses, or large windmill-like often found near the coast. The great
>
> of these is that they are clean and they will never run out (as long as the
>
> sun keeps and wind keeps blowing).

9 Compare with a partner and see if you have the same answers.

Listening and Summarizing

10 Listen to the CD. Write down information about renewable energy.

Questions / Renewable energy	The sun	Wind
Ways of harnessing energy		
Advantage		
Concern		

11 Listen again. Summarize what you have heard (either in Japanese or in English). Share your summary with your partner.

12 Read the entire passage. Compare it with what you understood when you listened to it for the first time in **3** at the First Listening.

The Future of Energy

On March 11, 2011, one of the strongest earthquakes ever recorded struck near the northeast coast of Japan. This was followed by a devastating tsunami, with waves as high as 10 meters sending seawater several kilometers inland. One of the many major consequences of this tragic natural disaster was that all electricity was lost at the Fukushima nuclear power plant. With no
5 electricity, it was not possible to cool down the nuclear reactors. As the world feared a major environmental and humanitarian disaster, the question everybody began to ask was "just how safe is nuclear power?"

As of March 2011, 14% of energy generated worldwide comes from 440 nuclear reactors in 30 countries. Some countries depend on it more than others; France, for example, gets 75% of its
10 energy from nuclear power, while Japan gets 29%. At the time of the earthquake and tsunami, Japan had two more nuclear plants under construction, and plans for at least 12 more to be built in the future. However, it is likely that plans to build more nuclear power plants, not just in Japan but in many countries worldwide, will be postponed at least until memories of the Fukushima plant begin to fade. That could be long in the future.

15 What, though, are the alternatives? The demand for energy grows and grows, while our supplies of oil, coal, and natural gas will not last forever. Perhaps the answer lies with renewable energy. In recent years, the use of renewable energy from natural sources such as the sun, wind, and oceans has become more and more widespread. Common examples of renewable energy are solar panels on the roof of houses, or large windmill-like structures often found near the coast.
20 The great advantage of these is that they are clean and they will never run out (as long as the sun keeps shining and wind keeps blowing).

It is not clear whether renewable energy can provide enough power by itself to support the growing modern world. However, with natural resources running out, and the world increasingly nervous of nuclear energy, every alternative needs to be seriously considered.

(352 words)

The Royal Wedding

Warm-up

1 Look at this picture. Discuss the question below with a partner.

House of Windsor

- George **V**
- Edward **VIII**
- George **VI**
- Queen Elizabeth **II**
- Princess Margaret
- Prince Charles
- Princess Anne
- Prince Andrew
- Prince Edward
- Sarah Ferguson
- Princess Camilla
- Prince William
- Prince Harry

☞ Who are the people in the blank boxes?

2 Work in groups of 4. Discuss the following questions.

a. Which of the following countries have a royal family? Circle the correct ones.

France   Holland   Thailand   the U.S.   Saudi Arabia

b. Ask members in your group whether they think royal families should be continued or not, and why they think so.

Name	Royal families should be continued	Why or why not?
ex. Yoko	Yes	They represent the country.

3 Listen to the CD once. Write down any key words you hear.

CD2
12

4 Discuss what you were able to catch with your partner.

Vocabulary

5 Work in pairs. First, use a dictionary and complete the chart below by yourself. Then, check the answers with your partner. Put a check (✔) in the box if you answered correctly.

English	Japanese	✔
spectacular		
tie the knot		
taint		
mend		
republic		
Japanese	**English**	**✔**
評判		
王位		
前妻		
非難		
廃止する		

Retention

Work in pairs. Student A does #1 and 2 and Student B does #3 and 4 in the following two tasks.

 6 Read each sentence and then repeat it with the book closed. Write down the number of times you had to read it until your partner decided you could repeat it correctly. Take turns with your partner.

1. It might be easy to forget the many troubles the Royal Family have faced in modern times.

2. In addition, over the years several negative stories have further tainted the royal reputation.

3. The Royals will be hoping, then, that this wedding will go some way to mending their public image.

4. There is a significant group in the U.K. that believes the Royal Family should be abolished.

Sentence	1	2	3	4
Number of times				

 7 Listen to each sentence and then repeat it. Write down the number of times you had to listen until your partner decided you could repeat it correctly. To check your partner's repeating, Student A should look at page 102 and Student B at page 106.

Sentence	1	2	3	4
Number of times				

8 Several words are missing in the following paragraph. Listen to the CD and identify where. Make a slash (/) where a word is missing and write the missing word below the slash. The first answer is done for you.

The wedding of Prince William of / and Catherine Middleton (now the

ex. Wales

Duke and Duchess of Cambridge) on April 29, 2011, was a spectacular.

Just for the ceremony in Westminster Abbey, 1,900 guests were present to

the popular young couple "tie the knot." More than one million people

took to the streets of London to, there were thousands of parties across the

country, and an three billion people—almost half the global—watched it

worldwide. The day was even made a national holiday to the event.

After learning this information, and after seeing on television the scenes in

London, it might be easy to forget the many troubles the Royal Family

have faced in times. In fact, various have seriously damaged their

reputation.

 9 Compare with a partner and see if you have the same answers.

Listening and Summarizing

10 Listen to the CD. Write down the problems the Royal Family have faced in modern times.

Who ?	What did he/she do?

11 Listen again. Summarize what you have heard (either in Japanese or in English). Share your summary with your partner.

12 Read the entire passage. Compare it with what you understood when you listened to it for the first time in **3** at the First Listening.

The Royal Wedding

The wedding of Prince William of Wales and Catherine Middleton (now the Duke and Duchess of Cambridge) on April 29, 2011 was a spectacular occasion. Just for the ceremony in Westminster Abbey, 1,900 guests were present to witness the popular young couple "tie the knot." More than one million people took to the streets of London to celebrate, there were
5 thousands of street parties across the country, and an estimated three billion people—almost half the global population—watched it worldwide. The day was even made a national holiday to mark the event.

After learning this information, and after seeing on television the extraordinary scenes in London, it might be easy to forget the many troubles the Royal Family have faced in modern times. In
10 fact, various controversies have seriously damaged their reputation. Some people still alive today will remember the great scandal in 1936 when Edward VIII gave up his crown so that he could marry a twice-divorced American woman (everyone probably knows the story even today, thanks to the movie *The King's Speech*). Since then, there have been many instances of affairs and divorces within the Royal Family, most infamously those of Prince William's own parents,
15 Charles and Diana. In addition, over the years several negative stories have further tainted the royal reputation: Prince Harry dressing in a Nazi costume; Sarah Ferguson (ex-wife of Prince Andrew) offering a meeting with her ex-husband for 500,000 pounds (about 70 million yen at the time); and the perhaps unfair accusation that the Queen acted inappropriately immediately following Diana's death.

20 The Royals will be hoping, then, that this wedding will go some way to mending their public image. This is actually very important, since there is a significant group in the U.K. that believes the Royal Family should be abolished. Between 13% and 22% of the population believe the U.K. should be a republic (the number varies depending on the level of scandal involving the Royal Family). Even if their public image doesn't improve that much, perhaps the two billion pounds
25 (about 260 billion yen) the wedding is expected to generate for the U.K. economy—thanks to increased tourism—will help people feel better about the Royal Family.

(366 words)

Hazards and Disasters

 1 Look at this picture. Discuss the question below with a partner.

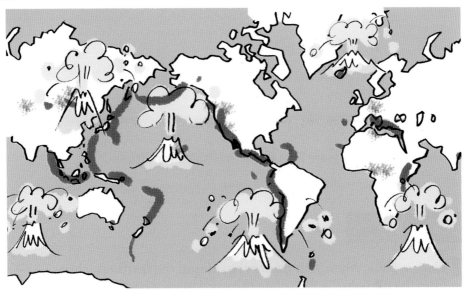

Name some countries that have many volcanoes.

2 Discuss the following questions:

a. Work in pairs. Out of 47,000 flora and fauna that the IUCN (International Union for Conservation of Nature) investigated, how many species are close to extinction? Circle the closest figure.

| 100 | 1,000 | 7,000 | 10,000 | 17,000 |

 b. Work in groups of 4. Think of endangered animals and write them down in the list below.

Endangered Animals
ex. Gorilla

First Listening

3 Listen to the CD once. Write down any key words you hear.

CD2
17

4 Discuss what you were able to catch with your partner.

Vocabulary

5 Work in pairs. When your partner has closed the textbook, choose a word from the list below and explain the word to your partner. Do not say the word itself or the Japanese translation. When your partner has guessed the word, switch roles. Put a check (✔) if you can give the correct word.

Words	日本語の意味	✔
volcano	火山	
inhabited area	居住地域	
earthquake-resistant	耐震設計の	
malice	悪意	
negligence	手抜き	
ensue	後に続いて起きる	
oil slick	油膜	
ecological	生態学的な	
extinction	絶滅	
flora and fauna	動植物	

Reproduction and Interpretation

Work in pairs. Switch with your partner when one of you has finished the
following two tasks.

6 Listen to the CD. First, Student A repeats the first part after the
beep, and then Student B repeats the second part. To check
your partner's repeating, Student A should look at page 102
and Student B at page 107.

7 Listen to the CD again. This time, interpret the phrases after the
beep into Japanese. Check with your partner.

Dictation

8 Several words are missing in the following paragraph. Listen to the CD and identify where. Make a slash (/) where a word is missing and write the missing word below the slash. The first answer is done for you.

These can be / divided into two kinds: natural and anthropogenic
      ex. further

(manmade). Natural hazards are, as the name suggests, of nature. The

hazard itself cannot be controlled by, although its effects can. Thus,

earthquake-resistant buildings can a hazard from becoming a disaster.

Unfortunately, it is often the case that the of nature is too strong, and no

amount of can stop disaster. The tragic Tohoku earthquake and tsunami in

2011 are of this.

9 Compare with a partner and see if you have the same answers.

Listening and Summarizing

10 Listen to the CD. Write down the answers.

Anthropogenic Hazards

Caused by	
Examples	(deliberately by humans)
	(not deliberately)

Anthropogenic Environmental Disasters: *Oil Spill*

When did it happen?	
Where did it happen?	
How much oil was released?	
How big was the oil slick?	

What kinds of hazards have humans created?

11 Listen again. Summarize what you have heard (either in Japanese or in English). Share your summary with your partner.

Post-Listening

12 Read the entire passage. Compare it with what you understood when you listened to it for the first time in **3** at the First Listening.

Hazards and Disasters

There is a difference between a hazard and a disaster. A volcano, for example, is a hazard, but not necessarily a disaster. If a volcano erupts in an uninhabited area, there are probably no (or few) severe consequences. Disasters happen when hazards—volcanoes, hurricanes, landslides and so on—strike inhabited areas that are not prepared to deal with them. The influence of a hazard, in
5 particular on humans, is what counts as a disaster.

These can be further divided into two distinct kinds: natural and anthropogenic (manmade). Natural hazards are, as the name suggests, events of nature. The hazard itself cannot be controlled by humans, although its effects can. Thus, earthquake-resistant buildings can prevent a hazard from becoming a disaster. Unfortunately, it is often the case that the force of nature is too strong,
10 and no amount of preparation can stop disaster. The tragic Tohoku earthquake and tsunami in 2011 are proof of this.

Anthropogenic hazards, on the other hand, are the direct result of human activity, especially mistake, malice, and negligence. The disasters that might ensue can be every bit as devastating as those caused by natural hazards. Terrorism and war are just two examples of how wide-ranging
15 disasters can be directly and deliberately caused by humans. More often it is not deliberate, for example plane crashes, mining accidents, and bridge collapses.

Anthropogenic environmental disasters are often in the news in recent times. In 2010, the Deepwater Horizon oil spill released about 800 million liters of oil into the Gulf of Mexico, creating an oil slick of at least 6,500 km^2 (approximately three times the size of Metropolitan
20 Tokyo). The ecological consequences of this will continue to be felt for many years to come. Another example is Chernobyl, the effects of which are still considerable even 25 years on.

The hazards we create affect the world around us. We are responsible for, among many other things, the earth's changing climate, for the extinction of countless species of flora and fauna, and for the fact that 60% of the ocean's coral reefs are at risk. We absolutely must think deeply about
25 how we, as a society and as individuals, can minimize the hazards, and prevent the disasters.

(367 words)

The Purpose of Language

Warm-up

 1 Look at this picture. Discuss the questions below with a partner.

How many people on earth do you think can communicate in English?

How much information on the Internet do you think is written in English?

 2 Work in groups of 4. Discuss the following questions.

a. Ask members in your group if they think they will need English in the future and ask why they think so.

Name	Do you think you will need English in the future?	Why or why not?
ex. Shun	Yes	A company I want to work for has designated English as their official in-house language.

First Listening

3 Listen to the CD once. Write down any key words you hear.

CD2
22

4 Discuss what you were able to catch with your partner.

Vocabulary

5 Work in pairs. First, use a dictionary and complete the chart below by yourself. Then, check the answers with your partner. Put a check (✔) in the box if you answered correctly.

English	Japanese	✔
means		
practical		
responsible for		
pleasure		
likely		

Japanese	English	✔
一般的に		
抽象的な、理論上の		
応用		
作業、雑用		
第一に、主として		

Retention

Work in pairs. Student A does #1 and 2 and Student B does #3 and 4 in the following two tasks.

 6 Read each sentence and then repeat it with the book closed. Write down the number of times you had to read it until your partner decided you could repeat it correctly. Take turns with your partner.

1. English stops being a means of communication, a tool to enable people to understand each other.

2. That's the reason more than one billion people worldwide speak English, either as their first or second language.

3. They are examples of the practical things language and communication are primarily intended for.

4. If you never use English, you will likely never properly learn it in the first place.

Sentence	1	2	3	4
Number of times				

7 Listen to each sentence and then repeat it. Write down the number of times you had to listen until your partner decided you could repeat it correctly. To check your partner's repeating, Student A should look at page 103 and Student B at page 107.

Sentence	1	2	3	4
Number of times				

Dictation

8 Several words are missing in the following paragraph. Listen to the CD and identify where. Make a slash (/) where a word is missing and write the missing word below the slash. The first answer is done for you.

What is the / of taking English courses? Many people in high schools,

    ex. purpose

universities, and companies Japan might give similar answers: to pass an

exam, to pass a class in order to graduate, to get a, and so on. Sadly, this is

the of living in Japan—you do need to pass English exams if you want to

graduate, or go to university. The problem is that it people to think of

English, or language learning in general, in the way. English stops being a

means of communication, a tool to enable people to understand each

other, and becomes an abstract test; something that will help you move to

the next of your life, but has no practical application in everyday life. This

is responsible for the fact that there are so many Japanese people, even

those in top universities, who have a good of English grammar and

vocabulary but cannot themselves clearly in the language.

 9 Compare with a partner and see if you have the same answers.

Listening and Summarizing

10 Listen to the CD. Answer the following questions. Share with your partner what you have written down.

CD2 26

1. What is possible through language?

2. What is an English expression quoted by the author? Write it down and explain what it means.

English expression	
What it means	

11 Listen again. Summarize what you have heard (either in Japanese or in English). Share your summary with your partner.

CD2 26

12 Read the entire passage. Compare it with what you understood when you listened to it for the first time in **3** at the First Listening.

The Purpose of Language

What is the purpose of taking English courses? Many people in high schools, universities, and companies throughout Japan might give similar answers: to pass an entrance exam, to pass a class in order to graduate, to get a promotion, and so on. Sadly, this is the reality of living in Japan—you do need to pass English exams if you want to graduate, or go to university. The problem is
5 that it leads people to think of English, or language learning in general, in the wrong way. English stops being a means of communication, a tool to enable people to understand each other, and instead becomes an abstract test; something that will help you move to the next stage of your life, but has no practical application in everyday life. This is largely responsible for the fact that there are so many Japanese people, even those in top universities, who have a good knowledge of
10 English grammar and vocabulary but cannot express themselves clearly in the language.

This is a great shame. It removes much of the joy and pleasure of learning a language, making it feel like a necessary chore. In actual fact, the main purpose of learning a language should be so that you can use it. That's the reason more than one billion people worldwide speak English, either as their first or second language. Using a language can mean many different things. Of
15 course, speaking with others is using a language, but it is just one example. Reading a book or magazine in English, surfing the Internet to find interesting non-Japanese websites (something like 80% of the Internet is in English, only 3% Japanese), watching English movies (in English), writing Facebook messages and emails to English-speaking friends, even just checking the local English newspaper for anything interesting; these are all ways of using English, and they are
20 examples of the practical things language and communication are primarily intended for.

There is an English expression, "use it or lose it." It means that if you don't keep practicing a certain skill, you will soon forget it. The same is true of English, but there is something else you should remember: if you never use English, you will likely never properly learn it in the first place.

(378 words)

Sport and Money

Warm-up

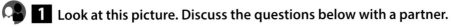 **1** Look at this picture. Discuss the questions below with a partner.

👉 Have you heard of the word "agent"?

👉 What do you think an agent's job is?

2 Discuss the following questions:

 a. Work in pairs. Can you think of differences between amateur athletes and professional athletes?

 b. Work in groups of 4. Think of amateur sports leagues and professional sports leagues in Japan.

Amateur Sports	Professional Sports
ex. Rugby	ex. Baseball

First Listening

3 Listen to the CD once. Write down any key words you hear.

CD2 27

4 Discuss what you were able to catch with your partner.

Vocabulary

5 Work in pairs. When your partner has closed the textbook, choose a word from the list below and explain the word to your partner. Do not say the word itself or the Japanese translation. When your partner has guessed the word, switch roles. Put a check (✔) if you can give the correct word.

Words	日本語の意味	✔
participation	参加	
enormous	莫大な	
earnings	収入	
exceed	上回る	
currently	現在	
effect	影響	
dedicate	専念する	
chase	追う	
loyalty	忠誠	
disappointing	失望させる	

Reproduction and Interpretation

Work in pairs. Switch with your partner when one of you has finished the following two tasks.

6 Listen to the CD. First, Student A repeats the first part after the beep, and then Student B repeats the second part. To check your partner's repeating, Student A should look at page 103 and Student B at page 107.

7 Listen to the CD again. This time, interpret the phrases after the beep into Japanese. Check with your partner.

Dictation

8 Several words are missing in the following paragraph. Listen to the CD and identify where. Make a slash (/) where a word is missing and write the missing word below the slash. The first answer is done for you.

The situation is quite different now. Broadcasters, / , and advertisers pay

[ex. sponsors]

enormous of money to sporting organizations, teams, and. The result is

that many professional players (people whose job is to play the sport) get

very high salaries. In 2009 Tiger Woods' earnings exceeded $1 billion

(about 80 billion yen), and football player Lionel Messi currently makes

more than $ (about 3.6 billion yen) each year. The average salary for a

Premier League football player in 2006 was pounds (about 140 million

yen at the time) per year. These are that most people can only dream of

making in their lifetime, let in one year.

---

 9 Compare with a partner and see if you have the same answers.

Listening and Summarizing

10 Listen to the CD. Write down the positive and negative effects resulting from the huge amount of money in modern sport.

Positive effects	Negative effects

11 Listen again. Summarize what you have heard (either in Japanese or in English). Share your summary with your partner.

12 Read the entire passage. Compare it with what you understood when you listened to it for the first time in **3** at the First Listening.

Sport and Money

It used to be that sport was something people did just for the enjoyment, or for the thrill of winning. Almost everybody was an amateur; that is to say, they did not receive payment for their participation. Until about 1988, professional athletes were not even permitted to compete in the Olympic Games.

5 The situation is quite different now. Broadcasters, sponsors, and advertisers pay enormous sums of money to sporting organizations, teams, and individuals. The result is that many professional players (people whose job is to play the sport) get very high salaries. In 2009 Tiger Woods' career earnings exceeded $1 billion (about 80 billion yen), and football player Lionel Messi currently makes more than $45 million (about 3.6 billion yen) each year. The average salary for a Premier
10 League football player in 2006 was 676,000 pounds (about 140 million yen at the time) per year. These are figures that most people can only dream of making in their lifetime, let alone in one year.

The huge amount of money in modern sport has positive and negative effects. In the past, amateur players needed to earn money by working other jobs. This meant they could not focus their time and energy on a sport. Now, professional players can dedicate all of their time to
15 becoming as good as possible. Also, because the financial rewards for success are so high, more and more people aim to become professional, making competition for the top places very strong. The result of this is that the level of the sport gets higher and higher. This makes the sport more popular, which attracts more broadcasters, sponsors, and advertisers, which of course makes more money for the sport and the players.

20 On the other hand, there are negative consequences. Most top players have an agent, and part of the agent's job is to get as much money as possible for the player. Players move from team to team "chasing the money," and traditional loyalty to one team disappears. This is disappointing for fans who stay loyal to their team their whole life. Furthermore, only richer teams and leagues can afford to pay the salaries of the best players, so the gap between a few teams at the top and
25 the rest widens.

Perhaps the biggest effect is the commercialization of sport. This can be seen in team names—for example, Rakuten Eagles and stadium names—for example, Arsenal's Emirates Stadium. Sporting schedules are changed to suit broadcasters, and in some cases even the format of a game is changed to suit advertisers. American teams are sometimes even referred to as "franchises."
30 Sport is no longer just about sport: it is an industry.

(445 words)

Japan's Aging Population

Warm-up

 1 Look at this picture. Discuss the question below with a partner.

 Which figures do you think show the average life expectancy of Japanese men and women respectively?

> 72   76   80   83   86   88

 2 Work in groups of 4. Discuss the following questions.

a. On average, women in which of the following countries have the most children in a lifetime?

> France   Kenya   the U.S.   South Korea   Cambodia

b. Ask members in your group what they would do to increase Japan's birthrate if they were Prime Minister?

Name	What they would do
ex. Tomoko	She would permit foreigners to work as domestic helpers or nannies.

First Listening

3 Listen to the CD once. Write down any key words you hear.

CD2
32

4 Discuss what you were able to catch with your partner.

Vocabulary

5 Work in pairs. First, use a dictionary and complete the chart below by yourself. Then, check the answers with your partner. Put a check (✔) in the box if you answered correctly.

English	Japanese	✔
life expectancy		
fertility rate		
account for		
pension contribution		
negative growth		
Japanese	**English**	✔
相対的に		
人口危機		
定年		
統計		
移民		

Retention

Work in pairs. Student A does #1 and 2 and Student B does #3 and 4 in the following two tasks.

6 Read each sentence and then repeat it with the book closed. Write down the number of times you had to read it until your partner decided you could repeat it correctly. Take turns with your partner.

1. Japan has long been known as a country whose citizens live for a long time.

2. Japan also has one of the lowest fertility rates worldwide, meaning that relatively few children are born.

3. In 2011, Japanese people aged 65 and older represented about 23% of the overall population.

4. It is thought that the Japanese population could shrink by a quarter by the mid-21st century.

Sentence	1	2	3	4
Number of times				

7 Listen to each sentence and then repeat it. Write down the number of times you had to listen until your partner decided you could repeat it correctly. To check your partner's repeating, Student A should look at page 103 and Student B at page 107.

Sentence	1	2	3	4
Number of times				

Dictation

8 Several words are missing in the following paragraph. Listen to the CD and identify where. Make a slash (/) where a word is missing and write the missing word below the slash. The first answer is done for you.

The long life expectancy is clearly something to be / , but what is the

        ex. *celebrated*

reason behind the birthrate? The main reasons appear to be the high cost

of and educating children in Japan, the fact that more women marry later

and enjoy careers, and that many Japanese people live in rather small

homes, not room for larger families. Whatever the reasons, the of not

somehow this trend are too serious to. By 2030, Japan could be

experiencing negative growth of 0.7% each year. With other countries'

and economies growing at such a fast rate, Japan needs to ask what it can

do not to get behind.

9 Compare with a partner and see if you have the same answers.

Listening and Summarizing

10 Listen to the CD. Write down the state of Japan's population in 2011 and what changes are expected in the near future if the current trend continues.

State of Japan's population in 2011	Changes that are expected in the near future

11 Listen again. Summarize what you have heard (either in Japanese or in English). Share with your partner what you have written down.

Post-Listening

12 Read the entire passage. Compare it with what you understood when you listened to it for the first time in **3** at the First Listening.

Japan's Aging Population

Japan has long been known as a country whose citizens live for a long time, and it still today enjoys the highest life expectancy of all countries in the world. On the other hand, Japan also has one of the lowest fertility rates worldwide, meaning that relatively few children are born. The result is that Japan is fast heading towards a serious population crisis—much of the country
5 is reaching (or has already reached) retirement age, and there are fewer people of younger generations to fill their place.

In 2011, Japanese people aged 65 and older represented about 23% of the overall population, while those over 75 years old accounted for 11%. If current trends continue, it is thought that the Japanese population could shrink by a quarter by the mid-21st century, 40% of which would be
10 made up of people older than 65. These are alarming statistics, and the cumulative effects could be quite significant. Already, changes are being felt in terms of government policy, and these can be expected to become more extreme. For example, you can expect taxes to be raised, pension contributions to steadily climb, and the age that you can finally stop working to be considerably older than 65—a U.N. report suggests Japan will need to raise its retirement age to as high as 77.
15 The same report also advises Japan to encourage much more immigration, aiming for as many as 50 million immigrants in the next half-century.

The long life expectancy is clearly something to be celebrated, but what is the reason behind the declining birthrate? The main reasons appear to be the high cost of raising and educating children in Japan, the fact that more women marry later and enjoy successful careers, and that many
20 Japanese people live in rather small homes, not allowing room for larger families. Whatever the reasons, the consequences of not somehow reversing this trend are too serious to ignore. By 2030, Japan could be experiencing negative growth of 0.7% each year. With other countries' populations and economies growing at such a fast rate, Japan needs to ask what it can do not to get left behind.

(359 words)

Appendix

Scripts for **Retention & Reproduction and Interpretation**

Student A

▶page 11

Unit 1 **The Rise of Social Networking**

Retention

3. Many people put too much personal information onto these sites.

4. It is quite possible that social networking will be a great benefit for humankind.

▶page 17

Unit 2 **The FIFA Football World Cup**

Reproduction and Interpretation

Today, /

it is one of the most watched sporting events /

on the planet, /

with more than a billion people /

tuning in to see /

at least /

some part of the 2010 final /

between Spain and the Netherlands. /

▶page 23

Unit 3 **"Cool Japan"**

Retention

3. The number of foreign students studying in Japan has increased sharply in recent years.

4. "Cool Japan" alone will not solve Japan's deeper economic problems.

▶page 29

Unit 4 **From Rags to Riches: A Story of J.K. Rowling**

Reproduction and Interpretation

Most of the writing was done /

in cafés in Edinburgh, /

simply because it was easier for her /

to get her baby to sleep /

when they were out /

of the small apartment /

they were living in. /

While her daughter was sleeping, /

Joanne was able to write. /

▶page 35

Unit 5 **Studying Abroad for Japanese University Students**

Retention

3. Some people argue that the trend outlined above is simply not true.

4. The future of this country falls on young people's shoulders.

▶page 41

Unit 6 **Stress in Modern Society**

Reproduction and Interpretation

These days, /

the word "stress" is more often used /

as another way to say /

we are busy, or nervous, /

or just uncomfortable. /

That's OK; /

languages change, /

and the meanings of words also change. /

However, we should not forget /

the original meaning of the word "stress," /

because what it creates is a serious problem. /

▶page 47

Unit 7 **Bankers' Bonuses: A Moral Issue**

Retention

3. Most people understood the need to save those key businesses.

4. Such measures have popular appeal, but they have also been criticized.

▶page 53

Unit 8 **Education in Singapore**

Reproduction and Interpretation

Also, many Singaporeans believe /

that the more educated they are, /

the more chances they have /

to succeed in their careers. /

The result is /

a highly efficient and effective education system /

that produces motivated and knowledgeable citizens. /

▶page 59

Unit 9 **Celebrities' Private Lives: Public Property?**

Retention

3. There seem to be three major reasons for this private life invasion.

4. We love seeing famous people, whether in a public or a private situation.

▶page 65

Unit 10 **The Future of Energy**

Reproduction and Interpretation

However, it is likely /

that plans to build more nuclear power plants, /

not just in Japan /

but in many countries worldwide, /

will be postponed /

at least until memories of the Fukushima plant /

begin to fade. /

That could be long in the future. /

▶page 71

Unit 11 **The Royal Wedding**

Retention

3. In fact, various controversies have seriously damaged their reputation.

4. Some people still alive today will remember the great scandal in 1936.

▶page 77

Unit 12 **Hazards and Disasters**

Reproduction and Interpretation

Disasters happen when hazards /

—volcanoes, hurricanes, landslides and so on— /

strike inhabited areas /

that are not prepared to deal with them. /

The influence of a hazard, /

in particular on humans, /

is what counts as a disaster. /

▶page 83
Unit 13 **The Purpose of Language**

3. There is an English expression, "use it or lose it."

4. If you don't keep practicing a certain skill, you will soon forget it.

▶page 89
Unit 14 **Sport and Money**

Reproduction and Interpretation **6 7**

Perhaps the biggest effect is /

the commercialization of sport. /

This can be seen in team names—for example, Rakuten Eagles /

and stadium names—for example, Arsenal's Emirates Stadium. /

Sporting schedules are changed to suit broadcasters, /

and in some cases /

even the format of a game is changed /

to suit advertisers. /

American teams are sometimes /

even referred to as "franchises." /

Sport is no longer just about sport: /

it is an industry. /

▶page 95
Unit 15 **Japan's Aging Population**

3. Changes are being felt in terms of government policy.

4. The same report also advises Japan to encourage much more immigration.

Student B

▶page 11

Unit 1 **The Rise of Social Networking**

1. Advertisers have also seen the possibility to reach millions of people easily.
2. Teachers use the sites as a convenient way to communicate with students.

▶page 17

Unit 2 **The FIFA Football World Cup**

The FIFA World Cup /
is one of the most important /
global sporting events. /
The first World Cup /
took place in 1930, /
and with the exception of /
1942 and 1946— /
cancelled due to World War II /
and its aftermath— /
the World Cup has been held /
every four years since. /

▶page 23

Unit 3 **"Cool Japan"**

1. The hope is that there will be two major benefits.
2. The Japanese economy will profit from increased sales and tourism.

▶page 29

Unit 4 **From Rags to Riches: A Story of J.K. Rowling**

Joanne Rowling was born in /
Gloucestershire, England, in 1965. /
In 1995, /
she was a single mother /
living in Edinburgh, Scotland, /

relying on state benefits /

to feed herself /

and her young daughter. /

At that time, /

she was writing a book /

based on an idea /

she had had five years earlier, /

in 1990, /

while sitting on a train. /

▶page 35

Unit 5 **Studying Abroad for Japanese University Students**

1. Young people are said to be indifferent to anything outside of Japan.

2. Internationalization has supposedly been promoted in Japan.

▶page 41

Unit 6 **Stress in Modern Society**

Reproduction and Interpretation 6 7

Stress. /

This is a word /

that has become very common /

in the modern world. /

You can often hear /

people say things like /

"I'm so stressed today," /

or "That was a stressful conversation." /

In fact, /

the word has become so common /

in the English language /

that it no longer has the same impact /

as it did before. /

▶page 47

Unit 7 **Bankers' Bonuses: A Moral Issue**

1. Certain banks and investors had become reckless and greedy.

2. The money was mostly in the form of repayable loans.

▶page 53

Unit 8 **Education in Singapore**

Singapore is a society /

that emphasizes academic qualifications. /

The government believes /

that since the country does not possess /

any natural resources, /

the population is the principal resource /

and must therefore be well-educated. /

▶page 59

Unit 9 **Celebrities' Private Lives: Public Property?**

Retention

1. Many celebrities *want* their pictures taken.

2. Is it OK to deliberately provoke a celebrity?

▶page 65

Unit 10 **The Future of Energy**

As of March 2011, /

14% of energy generated worldwide /

comes from 440 nuclear reactors /

in 30 countries. /

Some countries depend on it more than others; /

France, for example, gets 75% of its energy /

from nuclear power, /

while Japan gets 29%. /

At the time of the earthquake and tsunami, /

Japan had two more nuclear plants under construction, /

and plans for at least 12 more /

to be built in the future. /

▶page 71

Unit 11 **The Royal Wedding**

Retention

1. More than one million people took to the streets of London to celebrate.

2. The day was even made a national holiday to mark the event.

▶page 77
Unit 12 **Hazards and Disasters**

 Reproduction and Interpretation

There is a difference /

between a hazard and a disaster. /

A volcano, for example, is a hazard, /

but not necessarily a disaster. /

If a volcano erupts in an uninhabited area, /

there are probably no (or few) severe consequences. /

▶page 83
Unit 13 **The Purpose of Language**

Retention **7**

1. It removes much of the joy and pleasure of learning a language.

2. Using a language can mean many different things.

▶page 89
Unit 14 **Sport and Money**

Reproduction and Interpretation **6 7**

It used to be /

that sport was something people did /

just for the enjoyment, /

or for the thrill of winning. /

Almost everybody was an amateur; /

that is to say, /

they did not receive payment for their participation. /

Until about 1988, /

professional athletes were not even permitted /

to compete in the Olympic Games. /

▶page 95
Unit 15 **Japan's Aging Population**

 Retention

1. The result is that Japan is fast heading towards a serious population crisis.

2. 40% of which would be made up of people older than 65.

クラス用音声CD有り（非売品）
教師用音声CD有り（非売品）

Did You Catch It? [Text Only]
—Developing Skills in Listening
リスニング力を伸ばす集中トレーニング

2012 年 1 月 20 日　初版発行
2024 年 8 月 20 日　Text Only版　第 1 刷

著　　者　米田みたか、Chris Valvona
発 行 者　松村達生
発 行 所　センゲージ ラーニング株式会社
　　　　　〒 102-0073　東京都千代田区九段北 1-11-11 第 2 フナトビル 5 階
　　　　　電話　03-3511-4392
　　　　　FAX　03-3511-4391
　　　　　e-mail: eltjapan@cengage.com
　　　　　copyright © 2012 センゲージ ラーニング株式会社

装　　丁　㈱興陽社
組　　版　㈱興陽社
編 集 協 力　WIT HOUSE
　　　　　　ウィット　ハウス
本文イラスト　おぐらきょうこ
印刷・製本　株式会社エデュプレス

ISBN 978-4-86312-411-0